The Yearning Heart

Poems of Contemplation and Stillness

Hilary K Sinclair

Limitless

My boundaries reach beyond sisterhood,
Looking for a commonality of purpose
An explosion of joy,
That will shatter this sad world into stillness.

AuthorHouse™ UK
1663 Liberty Drive
Bloomington, IN 47403 USA
www.authorhouse.co.uk
Phone: 0800.197.4150

Published by AuthorHouse 07/26/2018

ISBN: 978-1-5462-9546-4 (sc)
ISBN: 978-1-5462-9547-1 (e)

Library of Congress Control Number: 2018908582

Print information available on the last page.

*Any people depicted in stock imagery provided by Getty Images are models,
and such images are being used for illustrative purposes only.
Certain stock imagery © Getty Images.*

This book is printed on acid-free paper.

authorHOUSE®

Contents

New Grace 11

Time Tunnel 13

Enlightenment Intensive 15

Limitless 17

Galaxies 19

Falling 21

Countryside 23

Spring 25

Butterflies 27

Déjà vu 29

Christmas 31

Grenze 33

Nelson 35

Oil 37

Floating, Singing 39

Poems with a Christian Connection 41

    Easter Morning 43

    PINK ROSES 45

    Seawall at Othona 47

    Beginnings 49

    Epitaph of an Enneagram 51

Refract the Lens of Time 53

    Mayhem's Gate: Post 9/11 54

    Mayhem's Gate 56

    Furnace 59

    Brass Ceiling 60

Preface

It has taken me ever since my first poem in 1977 until now (2017) to even think about publishing this very small collection of poems. But now, upon re-reading them I feel they may speak to an equally small number of people, whose spirits may be lifted by sharing in these very private yet also universal experiences. Certainly when I read them again recently I felt an astonishing kinship with them, as they spoke to me afresh from the great unknown. I have consequently left most to speak for themselves without embellishment, only adding a historical comment where this illuminates a poem in a new way, perhaps adding an explanatory context to it.

If anyone would like to contact me, my email address is:

sinclair.hk@gmail.com

Dedication

I dedicate these poems to the memory of my English teacher, Kathleen Flint, who fifty years ago introduced me to Emily Bronte, John Keats, Simone Weil, and a realm of mystical inspiration which began my still very incomplete journey. Also in grateful thanks to Rev David Bick, whose profound wisdom and reliable witness sustained me through many turbulent years. A few of these poems were written in the warm and friendly atmosphere of Wotton -under-Edge writers' group, helping me with inspiration and discipline.

I have appended an afterword for some of these poems, giving a little background to their creation. Others came 'out of the blue'.

Acknowledgments

I am thankful for the continuing work of the Clinical Theology Association, founded by Frank Lake in the sixties, and now called The Bridge Pastoral Foundation. Their ground breaking work in re-experiencing birth and neonatal trauma was pivotal for me. (www.bridgepastoralfoundation.org.uk)

Also for the regression work so brilliantly orchestrated by Simon Myerson in a group setting. (Previously of the Tavistock Clinic)

Many thanks to Pixabay, a brilliant copyright free photo archive, from where I sourced most of the photos accompanying these poems. Pixabay can be found at www.Pixabay.com

O clear the mind

Let it be blank

A white sheet, blank parchment,

Curl, uncurl softly.

No to lethargy – tranquillity –

How to fight the one and achieve the other.

New Grace

New grace, new space, new year

Make a place, make a place.

What is unknown will softly unfold

In the womb of time.

Truth is always only now-

The eternal moment, pure and

Without blemish,

Surrender to it, and be glad

© Hilary Sinclair 1976

Time Tunnel

I am long drawn out into the tunnel of time;

Aimlessly wandering through uncharted darkness,

infusing a soft sad glow,

growing incandescent with pain.

Perhaps one day I'll return to my own centre and know the truth.

The hollow core of loneliness is universal,

The remedy only is uniquely loving.

Enlightenment Intensive

I have trodden in the vacant interstellar spaces

I have frozen in the hub of the universe

The sound of stillness is in my soul.

I have heard the silence of a hawthorn tree

I have felt the trembling cracking of its branches

I know its strength and its fragility.

I have seen hope and love shine from another's face

I have been transfixed by love, and felt another's doubting agony

I have met another across infinite space.

Limitless

My boundaries reach beyond sisterhood,

Looking for a commonality of purpose

An explosion of joy,

That will shatter this sad world into stillness.

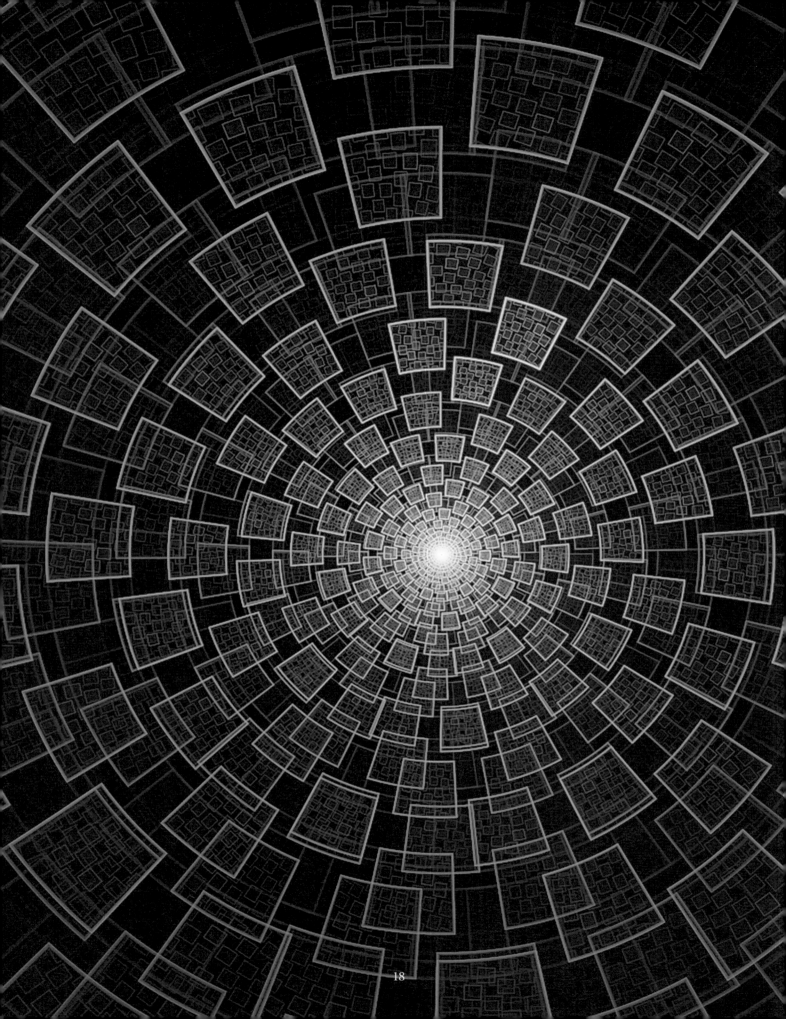

Galaxies

The superstructure of the galaxies is modelled in man's mind

His interwoven consciousness among the stars.

"Looking through a glass onion"*

-not peeled, but shattered painfully,

The pathway to the soul is resonant with life.

*Lennon/ McCartney quote.

Falling

The shackles clicked, quick as a flash

The neat nylon pink and blue ropes flickered like demented butterflies

Bounced, bounded, streamed through the cleats,

Plunging down the face of the rock

Taking me with them.

The world spun sideways,

My body shuddered, cavorting in empty space.

Abruptly, explosively, the belays took the strain

Holding the rope taut.

My safety.

The view was amazing.

Countryside

The cerulean canopy arches over the quiet landscape,

Tall larches leap, reaching upwards to the sky,

The trees trickling down a faint summer's sun.

Green glowing grass comforts a chubby rabbit,
surprised eyes inquisitively roving.

In gathering dew, smaller still, the slugs uncurl,

Intent on their evening roaming.

The river ferments under the ancient stone bridge

The throaty bleat of a distant sheep seizes the still air.

The harmony of England at rest holds us in thrall.

Spring

The crocus cracks the cold unforgiving ground

Its spike spears the implacable earth

While yellow daffodils yawn at the pale sun.

Torrents tumble over the stone overhang

Plunging into the clear pool.

White mist rises, a silent cloud,

Witness to a wet Spring

And the falling rain.

Soon summer blossoms melt our hardened hearts

And blooms assail our heightened sense

With fragrances of long ago.

Butterflies

Summer ends suddenly, butterflies all gone,

beautiful wings collapsed into dusky husks

dewlit grass, calm and clear

But what of the lonely, the old ones

querulously hunched over twilight fires,

Like the butterflies they too will have their end.

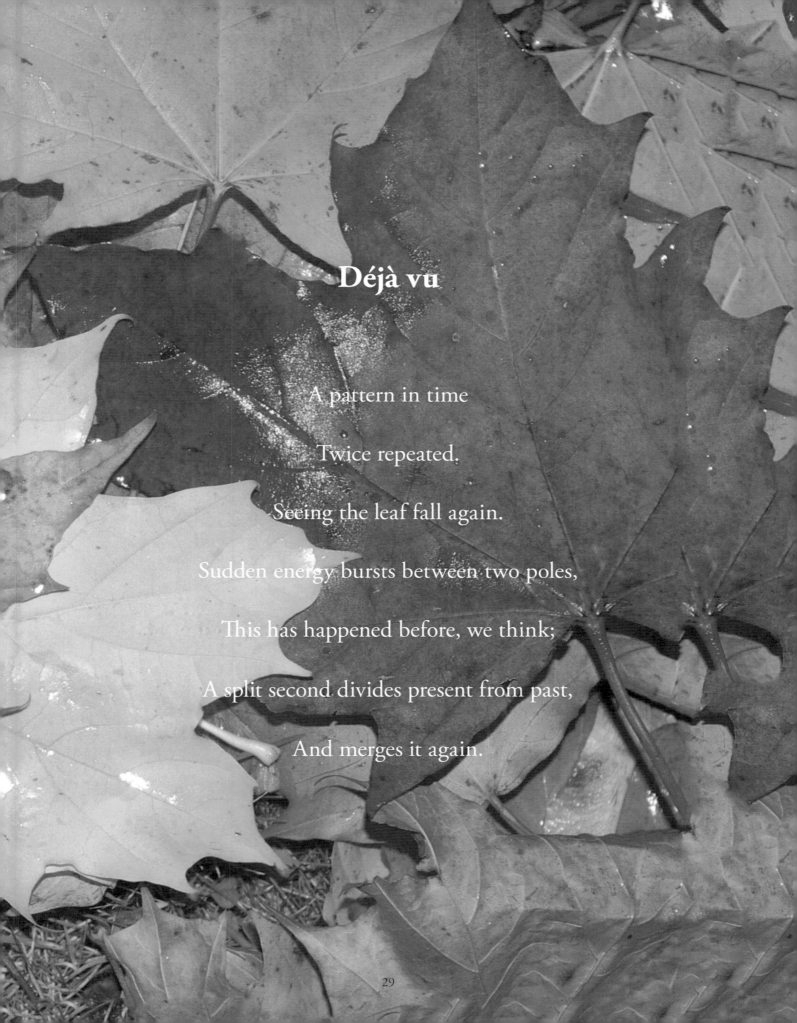

Déjà vu

A pattern in time

Twice repeated.

Seeing the leaf fall again.

Sudden energy bursts between two poles,

This has happened before, we think;

A split second divides present from past,

And merges it again.

Christmas

Christmas

Is not to conceptualise a meaning, rather know a truth,

Continuity of friendship,

Superficiality of contact,

Just nodding acquaintance,

Making up for lost time.

Christmas

Is sharing the joy of children,

Forgetting frustration,

Looking for a meaning;

Life is extreme in its demands.

Christmas

Clockwork roundabout of the seasons,

Rebelling against cottonwood Father Christmases

And bloated plastic clowns.

The sugar coated bitter pill of another year gone.

Accepting what is.

Grenze

Yellow, red and black,

Each post stands in the land,

Stands proud before an industrial strength fence:

Tall sentinels of alien pain.

A nation enslaved,

Trenchant history in time remembered

Soldiering on through lost campaigns:

The unsuccessful conclusion of a failed experiment.

A swathe of churned up earth morphs into the distant mist

And on the sentry towers

Embittered soldiers loll with vacant eyes.

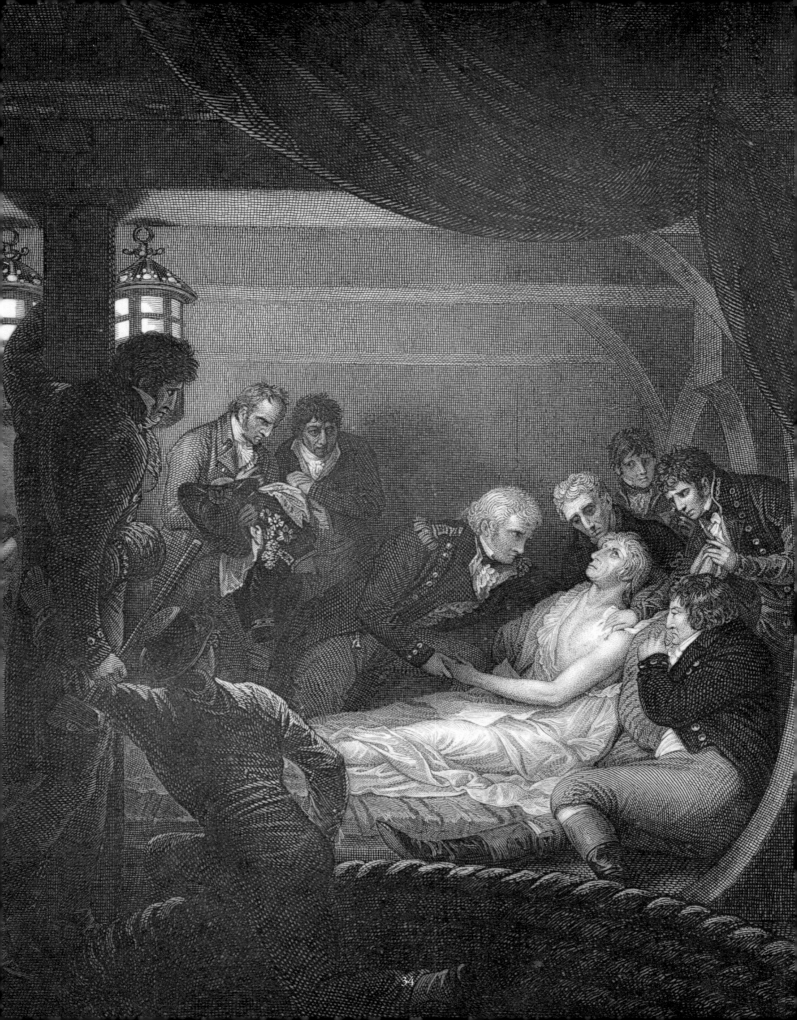

Nelson

Ships nestle like flies

Cradled on the sun-splashed water

Canon cock their muzzles, their black throats afire

Suddenly a canon roars, a musket flashes

Nelson hits the deck

The memory is etched, frozen in time

The image of a dying man

And the monumental churning of the sea.

Oil

The scowling cloud erupts, acrid portent from the burning sand

Noxious, routinely black smoke rises where the

Oil gushes gashes from a parched earth

Implicating us in its frenzied quest for fodder.

Seagulls squawk with raucous fervour

Ignorant of imminent death

Floating, Singing

Not the message, not the context,

But the pure voice of pain.

Out of the hurting, haunting void

Hurtles the sound of being,

Floating, singing,

The echo of a more satisfactory world.

Poems with a Christian Connection

Easter Morning

Transported through time,

On the edge of the future

I stand

Teetering on the brink of a new beginning.

Eternity stretches behind and before.

The bird of light lifts wings of wonder,

Soaring into the still air.

Go with him

for he will not land again.

PINK ROSES

PINK ROSES out of heavenly ardour blown

Blossoming from the humid earth;

What bright dewdrops reflect your holy face

And falling, mingle with the grass fresh mown.

(We know you're on the case.)

A promise of perfumed petals sown,

Brings a blush of profusion

A swell of lush confusion, comforting strained muscles in my heart.

In this soft stream of being my senses re-orient,
reform and poise themselves for truth.

Why can't truth be gentle like the roses?

Seawall at Othona

Stately white sails in gracious procession, far out in the estuary-

Beyond - the thin dark horizon, the bright blue sea.

Nearer, the obscurity of the mudflats - the

outward march of serried staves,

Marshalling the sand.

Eleven black barges silently guard the foreshore,

Sturdy barriers to the incoming tide;

The encroaching sand silts there, warding

off the power of the North Sea.

But the power of the silence is more commanding;

No sound of crashing wave

But only the soft blowing of the wind

Lifting us into the comfort of God

Beginnings

No beginning, no end; so says the Tao,

(But I believe in one point in created time when the world began)

At least I think I do.

Why is a point more scrupulous than an aeon?

Everything has a beginning; but does it have an end?

My beginning was at conception, or was it before?

A network of genetic formulae links me to the first man.

"As in Adam all die, so in Christ all are made alive."

"Before Abraham was, I AM, the shout of Jesus echoes down the years

A panegyric to time.

Epitaph of an Enneagram
"One"

Focusing on the One who is All

Not on the chaotic nightmare of the deep,

Surrounded by a pure circle of what is—

This could be bliss.

How to still the concatenating murmurs of disquiet

The frenzy of assessment, computation by the hour,

A summation of chaos which seizes

Constricts and narrows life.

Yes, my perfection, that for which I yearn,

Draws me steadfastly forward.

But the drawing out of the silent pool

Is hard to come by,

Existing only in a

Small piece of bread.

Refract the Lens of Time

Mayhem's Gate: Post 9/11

(Page One)

Refract the lens of time.

Hush into stillness the sun of centuries.

Too many memories lie verdant;-

the crimson gash of warring faiths

each swallowed by the dark maw, traitors' gate.

Those who believe the power is theirs

Theirs the ultimate of right

Must ride forever on its aching cusp.

Theirs the false belief, proclaimed as truth

Opening wide the gate to mayhem.

At Tyburn, Oxford, York, the Tower

The martyrs' blood still flows unceasingly-

That red bloom is the flower

That speaks of dogma's inhumanity.

It is a monstrous paradox

That any sound religion

Should turn itself upon its head

And exact an unforgiving retribution.

The sinews of hatred vibrate in a symphony of apocalyptic expectation.

The horsemen of Western capitalism

Ride roughshod across the plain.

Too late, too late the lament for latter day satanic mills

And for sharing our plunder with the poor.

Mayhem's Gate

(Page Two)

Those who believe the power is theirs,

Theirs the ultimate of right,

Must ride forever on its aching cusp.

Theirs the false belief, proclaimed as truth

Opening wide the gate to mayhem.

"You have heard that it was said,

'Eye for eye and tooth for tooth'.

But I tell you, do not resist an evil person.

If someone strikes you on the right cheek, turn to him the other also."

And now we walk as in a mist of unseen hfear

Fleeing the ghost of our own shadow selves,

Reluctantly embracing a world of inconstant uncertainty,

We brace ourselves for disaster.

"Find rest, O my soul, in God alone; my help comes from him."

Those who believe the power is theirs,

Theirs the ultimate of right,

Must ride forever on its aching cusp.

Theirs the false belief, proclaimed as truth

Opening wide the gate to Mayhem.

Furnace

From the furnace of pure gold

Flames ascend to the blue sky –

White hot the truth

That burns into the heart of man –

Brings fruit that ripens on the tree,

On the tree of Calvary

Brass Ceiling

The brass ceiling,

The impenetrable sky,

The leaden atmosphere,

All are sealing me off from the inflowing presence of God.

Where is the shaft of light spearing the darkness,

Swelling, possessing the black chasm of fear,

Rendering it impotent?

I look inside,

The rough fabric is scarred, clotted with blood.

(An angel speaks)

"It is not bright raiment we look for,

But a robe that envelops the great wound of the world,

A wound that pricks out lies and obfuscations,

secret malice and murderous intent,

that makes criminals, not martyrs, of us all."

Oh, but this is too much, too dramatic by far.

We would prefer to retire to our quiet firesides by

the telly and sip our Ovaltine in peace.

Don't speak of war and rumours of war.

But we cannot abort the process of destruction on our own;

We must live through it, embrace it and savour it.

How else can we find Him who is our peace?

(Finally, Our Lord says this)

Can you drink the cup which I drink and share the bread I give?

What will you surrender to the coming King?

End Notes

Enlightenment Intensive

The enlightenment intensive format, back in the seventies, enabled at that time some of the most stimulating, awareness producing, even mystical events in my life. During enlightenment intensives you may experience times of aching boredom, of tense frustration, of deadness and exhaustion.

There are moments of surging energy and great elation, experiences of universal laughter, and unique pain and grief, loneliness and isolation; truthful eloquence alternates with inarticulate dumbness and verbal diarrhoea. Inner chaos and tension gives way to equilibrium and meditative stillness.

Butterflies

I wrote this poem after coming home from taking my daughter to Primary School for her first day at school. Suddenly became aware of the finiteness of life.

Grenze

This was written in Duderstadt on an official visit with Stroud District Council, when we visited the frontier between East and West Germany. Two villages separated from each other by no man's land.

Nelson

A poem written in 2005 as part of the commemoration of the battle of Trafalgar.

Easter Morning

Written during the celebration of the Easter triduum led by Jim Cotter at Othona, Burton Bradstock.

Sea Wall at Othona

Written on the sea wall of the Othona community at Bradwell on Sea, Essex.

Epitaph for an Enneagram 'One'

Written during an Enneagram workshop at Emmaus House, Bristol.